Leveling the Aging Playing Field

Youth

old age

MIRIAM SAAM

Copyright @2021 by Miriam Saam

All rights reserved. No part of this book may be reproduced in any form or by any electronic or mechanical means, including information storage and retrieval systems, without permission in writing from the publisher, except by reviewers, who may quote brief passages in a review.

This publication contains the opinions and ideas of its author. It is intended to provide helpful and informative material on the subjects addressed in the publication. The author and publisher specifically disclaim all responsibility for any liability, loss or risk, personal or otherwise, which is incurred as a consequence, directly or indirectly, of the use and application of any of the contents of this book.

WORKBOOK PRESS LLC
187 E Warm Springs Rd,
Suite B285, Las Vegas, NV 89119, USA

Website: https://workbookpress.com/
Hotline: 1-888-818-4856
Email: admin@workbookpress.com

Ordering Information:
Quantity sales. Special discounts are available on quantity purchases by corporations, associations, and others.
For details, contact the publisher at the address above.

ISBN-13:   978-1-953839-75-6 (Paperback Version)
           978-1-953839-76-3 (Digital Version)

REV. DATE: 06/01/2021

Contents

My Aging Process And How It May Help You 2
My Appearance 5
Skiing 6
Old Friends 8
My Children 10
Life Is An Adventure 12
Aches And Pains 14
Move It, Or You Will Lose It 17
Obesity! 18
Make A Plan 21
Our Proverbial Shoe String 22
The First Toys We Owned 23
How We Got It All Together 24
My Housing Evolution 26
Money 29
Interesting Thing About Aging 31
On Being Unconventional 32
Politic And Religion 34
Let Go! 36
Labels 37
Diaries 38

This book is not written for the elderly to read, because I will never presume to advise the "Greatest Generation." They got this far without any help from me. It is written as a road map for the fifty something generations who wish to become successful in the aging game. This is a short book that is written by an elderly woman, who is young in mind and has reached her eighty-seventh birthday. I am that woman, although when I was fifty years old I had no idea, how I would get from that age to this point in time. When you hear an old person warn that you should cherish every moment of your young life now, because it all goes by so quickly, believe it. Prepare, not only by socking money in the bank, but deciding now how to live as an elderly person and enjoy those years fully. I am writing this book to alleviate some of the shock that comes when one day you look into your mirror and realize that you are no longer young. Being old can be a bonus, not a punishment.

Miriam Saam

*The year is 2015 and I am now 87 years old.
However, without undo stress, I do think
about dying, my own death, in particular.
This information will explain the following.*

MY SOUL

*What do I know of it?
Age claims my body, my candle glows dim.
Is it a reflection? A story grown thin.
Told by the Enlightened, again and again.
Dying, a fascination, as sand runs out,
Where, how, and when?
Answers in TIME, my time.
If there is nothing, then death does not matter.
Only by living, hope will not shatter.
I know, I must grow till then.
As life friends leave me, a thought ever follows.
They know the answer!
Amen.*

Written by Miriam Saam

My Aging Process
And How It May Help You

I am eighty seven years of age. I could write that statement in large black and underlined letters, and it really wouldn't matter. I could put them on a billboard, or have them dragged behind an airplane over Atlantic City and it just wouldn't make any difference to the young person that lives inside my head. That person is still wondering why the stair steps are growing in height and why, when I am down on my knees weeding the garden, I need the help of my hands on the ground to get me upright again. It is not a pretty sight. Just the other day I was in the middle of this process when a very nice man stopped his car on the road that is right next to my garden to ask me if I needed any help! Please don't get me wrong. It was a sweet gesture on his part, but I really don't want to be assisted by the proverbial Boy Scout who Helps the Old Lady cross the street. I still see myself as I have always been, young! Somewhere along the way I just didn't notice that I had been transformed into that old lady who insists on pushing her way into every mirror I look into. I know that I should be grateful for my good health and almost sharp mind, and I am. Just because I find myself standing in front of an open refrigerator door wondering just what I am looking for, it doesn't mean a thing. Everyone has done the very same thing no matter what age they are.

My mornings begins with my daily list, I write down the activities that I wish to accomplish. After they are finished I draw a black line through them. I truly think one of the problems of the aged is the lack of direction, mindless wandering through endless days of nothingness. Make each new day count; make it special. To do this takes effort. That effort is called living. Accomplishment is the part where the black line comes into the play. The simple activity of writing a list at the beginning of each day is exactly the way that the world works. It goes by many other names, but it is simply a list. Being an elderly person does not mean idleness. It only puts the effort of facing each new day directly upon you.

So get into this habit now. Cultivate the thought before you get old.

Doodles open up what is in your head

My Appearance

I do not wish to look like anyone else, so the tight helmets-like hair styles that many beauticians recommend for elderly women are out. I follow trends in fashion that appealed to me through the years. I have found ways to accent my good qualities and disguise the thing about myself that I do not wish to share. I recommend a mirror that shows your image from more than one angle. You may be surprised by the rear end view! I repeat myself; Do the best with what you have. Never worry about the unsolicited advice of others. You will only be the subject of their conversation until they find a new victim. When I've put too much time into worrying about what other folks, think. I stop, think and remember what someone said to me a long time ago. What other folks think doesn't pay my bills, and until they do, they can "BUZZ OFF."

Now is the time to invest in the mirrors for your bi-fold closet doors.

Knowing what to do before you get there is this book's only purpose.

Skiing

At the age of eighty, I found that skiing just wasn't fun anymore. The last time I stood at the top of a gently sloping hill, I began to think about the possibility of a fall, not so much about hurting myself as the embarrassing situation of not being able to get back up at least somewhat gracefully. Even as a much younger woman this activity had always been somewhat of a problem for me. I've thought about that and decided it may have contributed to my ability to stay upright on my skis. I felt better about the whole problem when I read an article in a *Ski Magazine* stating that it was a matter of a male-female center of gravity. My center had gone south a long time ago. At this point, I guess I should explain how an eighty-year-old woman had any business being on a ski slope in the first place. That is a long story that began back in 1944. An elderly neighbor, who in my young mind must have been at least forty years old, asked me to help her clean her garage. That job included climbing up onto a loft and that was where I found my first pair of skis. They were beautiful. When the job was finished, I accepted them as payment for my work. This began a love affair with the sport, that with the help of a local ski club, took my husband and myself to the Alps and beyond. When we joined the Lancaster Ski Club in the fall of 1956, we found that we were one of the few married couples who had a house and three small children. Our home was a ready-made place for our friends to meet, and on many occasions, party. Because the ski club was populated by many younger single members, we have always had younger friends. I have found this association has contributed in a very large way to my ageless view of life and the absence of the whole aging process, at least in my mind. Use young friends as your inspiration.

Old Friends

At this point I wish to expound on a "touchy" subject. OLD friends, can be depressing when there are just too many in one place. The discussion many times centers around who died, who is ill, their medications, how boring life is, and how lonely they are. To avoid the above situation, I recommend that you do not associate with old people, or even folks your own age. Just a minute before you have a hissy fit, let me exchange the word "old" for words like boring, or tiresome. Think about it, when at any age have you liked the company of the people I have just described. So why is it that the elderly will put up with them now? I submit that they never though about the possibility that they may outlive all of the great friends who filled their lives with the fun of just being alive. And now they may be left with the same people they never liked, before they got old. So before you get to my age, think about how great it can be to be old in body, but never in spirit. Your Spirit is one thing that will makes you into an interesting person, no matter what age you are. Begin to collect younger friends now, and you may be able to enrich their lives and your own as well.

Miriam Saam

Open a Window, Let Life In

My Children

 My children also were a great influence on my agelessness. I admit that my priorities when they were young didn't include my so-called house work as much as it did the games we played and the projects that filled most of our days. The house got a very fast once over about one hour before my husband was due to arrive home from work. Dinner wasn't a big problem either as I hadn't entered my gourmet phase yet. I remember almost as if it was yesterday the Arab tent I made by covering one of those square fold away rotary cloth line, with wide striped fabric. Then there was the mama doll that was bigger than my oldest daughter, who was seven years old when I made it. I really played with the kids, not only my own, but three more that I baby-sat for every week. My theory at the time was built upon the premise that all the neighborhood kids liked to play at my house anyway, so why not help another mother out who had to work, while at the same time helping to pay our bills. Money has never been abundant in our life, but we always managed to get just enough for what was important. Because I didn't have a real "job" until the children were older, I added to the family income with attempts to make extra money. We, meaning the kids and I made a game out of every crazy money making-scheme I could come up with. I remember dressing Amish dolls for some local gift shops. Drying pansies flowers and placing them under a curved glass to make a cute wall hanging, didn't exactly set the wall on fire. That project actually was a corporation named FLEURI CRAFT, and I was the president of the company. The farthest we got with that adventure was a sale to the B.Altman Co. In New York City and a very large add in the New York Times.

Life Is An Adventure

Most of my life has been an adventure of one kind or another and that is why age hasn't been accepted by me now, even though the calender says the years do not lie. So what do I do now? Join the local senior citizen's group and take swimming classes at the local pool? I never go out in public with my bare arms showing, let alone my own "not so lovely" behind. Do the best you can with what you have has always been a good way of approaching life. Just be who you are on the inside and the outside doesn't matter. I am young inside to the extent that I never really see the ageing process that is freely shown to everyone else until we talk. Then everything changes. If you have a true interest in the world you live in today and not the one you remember as the "GOOD OLD DAYS," many doors will open to an exciting world. I, at this time, have my limits. I do not Tweet, Twitter, or Text. If I find my E-mail doesn't work or my phone is dead, then, I may be forced to, look at the world around me. Who knows what I might find?

Getting back to the good old days, if my memory doesn't deceive me, they weren't so good. For many elderly people the problem is that memory is a selective thing. It emphasizes only the good and minimizes the bad. That attitude is a two-sided coin that deserves more attention. The family reunions, the spring wild flowers, the rides in the car to the country were all great memories, but Measles, Polio and Consumption, were accepted facts of life. The life span of the general population was so much shorter than it is today that the problems, of paying for your children's college and caring for aging parents didn't exist. Child birth carried a greater risk of death and a high infant mortality rate was also a reality. There are many other examples I could point out. I just wanted to make a point. The good old days were really not that good.

Aches And Pains

Why is it that aches and pains are synonymous only with old age? People have them at one time or another, even when they are children. The only thing that comes to my mind at this moment is when you reach an age when the discussion of your aches and pains become the center of your daily conversation. You have succumbed to the myth that you are old. There are many legitimate reasons for elderly people to be distressed, I am merely pointing out that many times their problem didn't begin when their age was obvious, but many years before when they treated their minds and bodies as trash cans. They greedily absorbed the fast foods and mindless pursuits of a sedentary life style, pursuit a beautiful tan that dries and wrinkles their skin, add added pounds that expanded waist lines. Look at yourself now and try to fast forward to your appearance in twenty years. I am not recommending plastic surgery, just common sense changes. If you were lucky enough to be born with a healthy body and good genes, as I was, the following advice is for you. First of all, be thankful and appreciate your good fortune. Show that appreciation by taking care of yourself. The world is full of people who have an uphill battle from the day they are born. If you want to understand just how fortunate you are take the time to visit a Goodwill Industry Workshop or a Veterans's hospital, a nursing home, mental hospital, soup kitchen or homeless shelter. The process of taking care of yourself ideally this should start when you are young, as many of the ills of old age begin with too many concussions received in the pursuit of a ball of some kind, or the undestroyable cloche the young wear that allows them to take risks that are unthinkable in later years.

Leveling the Aging Playing Field

Let the Music of the Past Fill your dreams

Move It, Or You Will Lose It

 If you do not move it, you will lose it! I am eighty seven years of age and just yesterday I relayed bricks in front of my garden shed after my son removed them and added a layer of gravel. The idea that I cannot do anything I set my mind to, has never entered my head. I have been told on many occasions that I am just too old to do many things. If I haven't figured this out for myself, my body has told me clearly that I cannot. For instance my diminished balance has said it is time to quit skiing when I was eighty years old. But working in my garden is something I can do, but with a lesser degree of gusto. I just take more rest periods between the jobs I am pursuing. Looking forward is another activity that can make your life worthwhile. Waiting for things to grow, watching seeds that you have put into the ground sprout and blossom are healthy signs of life. Tap the reservoir of the many years that are behind you. Write that poem. You know the one that has been hiding way in the back in your mind. Put your silly painting on canvas. Who is it that makes the decision about what is art? Write a book. Do whatever you can to make your life interesting, not only to yourself but to others around you.

Obesity!

The very first time I truly noticed the obesity explosion in this country was in the year 2000. The following week after returning home from a trip to Europe, my husband and I attended a picnic that was held at Hershey Park. I was shocked at the difference in the physical size of the general public between the Europeans and the Americans. I did not see any obese people in the countries we visited in Germany and France. Hershey Park was full of them! Why the difference? I asked myself. I had to know. I finally came to the realization that one of the answers was the different attitude that separates the Europeans from us. Eating in Europe is an art first and a necessity second. All of the shops closed at noon for lunch and did not reopen until two in the afternoon. This was a lesson I learned the first day we arrived in Frankurt, Germany, when I was unceremoniously escorted to the door of the store at exactly noon. Sidewalk Cafes were everywhere. Bright table cloths and enticing aromas invited all to sit down, relax and enjoy not only the food but the ambiance of the moment, usually topped off with a bottle of good wine. I am not suggesting that by any stretch of the imagination we can compete with the above description. I am only trying to find an excuse to explain the difference. Fast food is just what the name implies. It is fast, greasy, fattening and "Super Sized." We are eating ourselves to death. Lately this fact seems to be noticed by nutrition experts and educators who are training children to eat more nutritious lunches in school. Shows like "The Biggest Looser" are slowly turning up the heat on a subject that was considered indelicate and hurtful in the recent past. This show also makes it very clear that losing a lot of weight is one of the most challenging efforts anyone can try to do. If you are constantly aware of your weight, it cannot sneak up on you. Buy a scale. Let me show you how an experience of my own had made me painfully aware of a problem I had never encountered before. One hot summer day, we went to the Philadelphia Zoo, I decided that wearing a long summer skirt would be a good way to stay cool. Everything went well until I found that the inside of my upper thighs was causing me great discomfort. I certainly didn't consider myself to be fat, just a bit chubby. The friction caused by my legs encouraged me to find the nearest first aid station, where an attendant happily handed me the Talcum powder as I entered the door. It was half empty. I wasn't the first person to need it that day. I started to look at some statistics about the number of knee replacement surgeries that have dramatically increased lately and the decrease in the ages of the patients who need them. How many of these people are overweight? Good question, but it is impolite to bring that up.

The Old Man's Wine Glass is Filled with Memories

Make A Plan

    Young lovers often say that they want to grow old together. As the years go by, young people make many plans. They go to college, embark on a great career, travel the world, own a home, have a family. The list goes on and on, but they never even consider making a plan for the ultimate success of a happy old age. It doesn't just happen by accident. Just as any worthwhile project demands a plan, so does a happy ending. Remember the phrase about growing old together can only happen if you understand this activity takes planning. Busy lives often need to be slowed down to allow time to contemplate what comes next. Divide the times of your life into sections. Birth until twenty, is pre-adult or section one. Twenty to forty, is your family rearing years, or section two. Forty to sixty, are the years you begin to prepare for your coming old age. The popular idea is to accumulate enough money so that when we retire we can do all the wonderful things being freed from the restraints of the work allow. I do not recommend the following advice for everyone, I merely wish to tell you how my husband and I dealt with those years.

Our Proverbial Shoe String

 We lived like millionaires on the proverbial shoestring. We saved money wherever we could so, that we could spend it on the thing that really matter to us. We built a savings account of memories instead of money in our bank. Our first sailboat was an old wooden "Lightening." My husband had to completely fiberglass the hull in order to make it seaworthy. The date was nineteen-sixty-one. This began our adventure on the Susquehanna River. A few years later we joined two good friends and became partners in the rental of an old cabin on one of the islands on that river. Our family spent our summers, sailing, swimming, and living up to the reputation of all "good river rats." Our winters were also filled with activity. After my children were old enough, we all skied at Denton Hill Ski Area in northern Pennsylvania. We banked memories that will last longer than any amount of money. After our three children grew up and left the nest my husband and I expanded our horizon to include trips to ski areas in Europe, Canada and many western states. We decided to become home bodies when our balance became questionable. Why am I telling you about all of this? Because sometimes when we have the money, we do not have the physical ability to do the things we planned for.

The First Toys We Owned

Thinking back over the years, I often reminisce about the used Volkswagon bus that we bought in the nineteen sixties. Because it was so bizarre and the price was low enough to fit into our budget, we became its owner. The only description that truly fit is that of a home-made hippy vehicle. This adventure enriched our lives. Most campers begin the camping experience with a tent and cot. Not our family; we began fully equipped. We soon learned just how many things we did not know about camping! Our toy was the only vehicle we owned. A two-car family was way beyond our means. The point of all of this is to live life with a bit of panache, a sense of adventure, and the thrill of just being alive. When old age arrives, you never look back with regrets of opportunities missed.

How We Got It All Together

Many years ago as a child of the great depression, I was familiar with hand - me - down clothing. Everyone I knew was in the same boat, so you only stood out if you had something that was new. This habit stayed with me all of my life. The difference now is that I do it because it is fun. In the summertime we love garage sales. The rest of the year we shop in Goodwill stores and the Salvation Army. It is all about the thrill of the treasure hunt replacing the boring shopping mall experience. I know that this is not for everyone, especially a person who needs to impress others with the expensive store label that is attached to the bag the item is housed in.

Miriam Saam

See Beauty in All Things

My Housing Evolution

After our wedding in June of 1948, we lived in a small city apartment. We built our first small house in 1951. We managed to accomplish this by saving every cent of my wages and all benefit funds my husband received. from his naval service during World War II. My father-in law offered to match any amount of money we saved with a loan. With that much collateral a bank loan was assured. And the fun began, I searched everywhere for used items to fill our cute little house and we began our family. After three children and ten years had gone by, we needed more room and we also began thinking about my husband's parents moving in with us as they aged. We bought a large old house in the city that was built around the turn of the century. The furniture that once fit our little house so well, was too few in number and too small in size. Thus my search began again to fill it up with a brand new big house theme, using second hand items. The year was 1962 and what a wonderful and exciting time the next years were for the entire family. My two daughters met the men they loved, married and began families of their own. Although the wonderful old Victorian house didn't change, my husband, our son, Christopher, and I had. Due to a group of very interesting people I met when I took the position of program development director at our local GOODWILL, the sixties were for me a religious wakening. First and most important was my introduction to Edgar Casey and the Unitarian

Church. The minister became a part of our eclectic group of open-minded thinkers, all of whom were many years younger than my husband and myself. Now the big house was too big and too empty and no longer suitable for our new lifestyle. One day I told a co-worker who happened to live in southern Lancaster County that I would like to move there. This idea came clear to me mostly because of my job. I was hired to raise money and doing so require me to speak to church groups, business men, clubs, and to escort people through the GOODWILL workshop. By speaking to that many people, I got a very good feel for the different personalities I encountered. After a rather unsuccessful first year, I had to find a better way to approach my target. The idea came from a Goodwill newsletter item about some hippies in California that were found sleeping in one of the yellow five foot square collection boxes. The wheels in my head began to turn. A brand-new mall was just being finished in our town, and I convinced the owner to allow me to set up a yellow Goodwill collection box in the center court. It would have a sign on its roof announcing that "being disabled was like living in a box." I told him that this would get me the publicity I needed, but would also benefit the mall. He agreed and in 1971 I moved into the box and did not come out again for two weeks. I became "THE LADY IN THE BOX." The whole project was a great success and I repeated it again the next year. In November of 1972, we moved from our nine-room city house to a mobile home "way down in the sticks" on the most beautiful piece of land I had ever dreamed of. It had two spring-fed streams on it and was surrounded by woodland. Before we could move, I had to dispose of many of the pieces of old furniture from our big house. Many pieces had now become part of a new category. They were antique and had increased in value. I gave them to my oldest daughter to cherish and hand down to her children. Then in 1978, we sold the tailor and built our present home. The familiar of the antiques were now replaced with an interesting collection of eclectic furniture and exotic curios that boggle the mind of everyone who sees them. We added a second floor apartment to our house when it became obvious that we were both too old to care for such a large property. Our son, Chris, and his wife, Missy now live with us so that we may stay here in our final home on this planet.

Money

You would be surprised just how well two retirees can live on very little money. First of all we managed to own our home outright before we retired. When we run short of funds, our home acts as a life line to bails us out. Because neither my husband nor I ever had enough money to cause us to worry, we have always been frugal in our spending.

Fortunately my eyesight and hearing are still good. This allows me the mobility to drive the short distance to our local Amish supermarket. I always shop with a list, but add to it if a real bargain happens to appear. Anything that I need and cannot find there, takes me to my next stop at our local Dollar store. Finally, I shop at the much more expensive supermarket. Buy one and get one free bargains are a must have there.

Treasure Hunts are scheduled at least once a month at one of the three Goodwill stores in our area. I make it my business to know how important expensive labels are. When I sat in my doctors' office, I entertained myself reading fashion magazines. Since the down turn in the economy, the word cheap doesn't get such a bad rap. Summertime offers the fun of garage sales, that yield great bargains. I have a Jacuzzi on the deck that I bought at a garage sale! If you are a gardener, you understand the world that occupies my mind, any season that it happens to be at the moment. Tending my collection of beautiful African Violets keeps me happy on cold winter days. Spring offers the challenge and anticipation of new shoots pushing their way above ground. Weeding is one way of thinking about absolutely nothing.

Miriam Saam

Interesting Thing About Aging

The interesting thing I never considered about aging began one day when I pulled the car onto the side of the road in order to check directions on a map. To my complete surprise, a car stopped and the driver's passenger asked if my husband and I were alright. Did we need any help? We thanked them for their concern but said we were just reading a map. This isn't the best story I have concerning this subject. After we attended our daughters' birthday celebration, we left for home just a bit after midnight. I should stop right here and say I feel sure that if we were driving an approved "old people car" none of the following would have happened, but our mode of transportation was a very sporty 1983 Camero. With red lights flashing, a police car hailed us down and I pulled to the side of the road. The young boys-out-for-a-joy-ride look on the officer's face quickly faded to one that I am hard pressed to describe. When he heard the question, "how may I help you officer," coming from the proverbial little old lady in the drivers seat, the cop was astounded. Another amusing thing happened to me when I finished shopping in my local grocery store. With my packages in tow, I searched the parking lot for my 1983 bright red Camero. I found it surrounded by a group of young boys, who were obviously admiring it. To their surprise, this old lady took out her keys and got in and turned on the engine. Then they asked, "can you really drive a stick shift?" I didn't dignify the question with an answer. I just drove away.

On Being Unconventional

I didn't start out with the idea of being a strange sort of person. It just came naturally to me and I have found it to be a great asset. No matter how ridiculous my actions are, I am forgiven because I am an oddity in the rather conservative area where I live. I submit that if a normal person does something out of character, everyone is shocked, but if you have a reputation for being a little "off-the-wall", no one even notices. To illustrate this phenomenon, I will dredge up things that happened in my past that illustrates my point. Many years ago I decided that it would be fun to try my hand at fishing. How hard can it be? So I dug around in my old stuff and found a net and a fishing rod. It was okay, but it needed new line. I had great difficulty with this project, so using my lifetime experience with gerry rigging, I finally had my solution. I tied the end of the string to a post on the edge of our property and proceeded to walk down the road till I felt I had enough line to do the job. Then I began walking back, rewinding as I went. I should tell you that there are no close neighbors and my project took me through a mostly wooded area. A car filled with people drove by, I didn't wave as both of my hands were busy, I did notice faces staring out the window. A few weeks later I was trying to catch a young carp that my son-in-law had put in my small spring fed pond. I discovered its natural mud digging habit was something I disliked and the carp had to go. With net in hand I had just begun my effort when

Miriam Saam

I heard our black Lab barking. I went to see what the problem was and I found the dog had cornered a young pig in the stream. At approximately the same time a pick up truck arrived at the scene containing the pig's owner. I let the dog go. So he can help me get the pig back. The pig, the dog, the farmer and I, still holding the net in my hand, went running down the road. When the same car passed us, (at least the faces in the back window looked strangely familiar), So you see how much fun you've been missing. It's best to start early if you want to become a character in old age.

Politic And Religion

Just before we would leave the house to attend an outing, my darling husband would suggest that it would be a good idea if I refrained from discussing two of my favorite subjects - politics and religion. My answer was always the same. "What else is there to talk about?" "You may offend someone,", was his sweet-natured answer. I complied with his wishes, at least until I found a worthy opponent. Then all bets were off. When I find a person who is as passionate about the state of our country as I am no matter what their political persuasion, I thoroughly enjoy the back and forth banter and I have an excuse to use the news I collect every day from the local newspaper and the information I glean from various commentators on my television. Why am I bringing this up and what does it have to do with aging? My answer is keep up! Know what is going on now. Be interested and interesting. Have an opinion. Challenge others, and for God's sake, do not be boring. Anyone who is boring at any age is tiresome, but to be boring and old is twice as bad. And while I am speaking of God, my next subject is my own personal opinion. Upon seeing the stars in the universe, how can GOD's greatness be reduced to one religion? Christianity is but one of the worlds' great religions. Tolerance and understanding are very difficult to acquire. The many religious wars are evidence that societies may never obtain a reasonable way to live together. May I be so bold as to suggest believe what you will, but understand that you may not have all the answer. Don't try to inflict your belief on anyone who may not agree with your views. The framers of the Constitution knew what they were doing when they separated the church and the state. The Pilgrims came here for religious freedom. Try to respect others and their beliefs and remember they may be prejudiced against what you believe in. I am prejudiced against only one group of people. They are called bigots. ONE OBSTINATELY OR INTOLERANTLY DEVOTED TO HIS OWN CHURCH, PARTY, BELIEF OR OPINION.

Let Go!

Dwelling on past family disagreements is nonproductive at best, and totally disabling at worst. After trying to solve a problem and reaching a stalemate, stop trying to fix it. Go on with your own life and allow the other members of the family the freedom to go on with theirs. Any relationship with you should be because they want to be with you, not because they must. An obligation is not what you ever want to be. Realize the young family you remember of many years ago has outgrown the need for your council. They have their own lives and you become less needed every year that passes. Understand that doesn't mean this is a deliberate action to hurt you, but it is just reality. After you became a young adult, think back to the times that you visited your own elderly relatives. Why were you visiting them? Were you there because you really wanted to see them? Were you feeling guilty? Children love to visit grandparents They are an important part of their growing up years. Remember as they grow and their lives become more crowded with activities, their interests widen far beyond the milk and cookie stage. One of the major errors that are often made by the elderly is reminding their visitor just how long it has been since their last visit. By doing so, you have immediately put them on the defensive. Obligatory visits are of no benefit to either of you.

Labels

We received a label the second your father put his sperm in your mother and you are a fetus. Then we receive a new label for every step of our march to adulthood. We are a newborn a baby, a child, a preteen, a teenager, a young adult, and finally, a fullblown adult. "Whew!" Now we head the other way. Young adult, middle age, an elderly person, and finally old. Notice this last list seems too short to cover all the nuances that determine each age, especially the one on middle age. I am concentrating my effort in this book on middle age first as a precursor to old age. Make up your own label now, or someone will hang another less flattering one on you later. While I am discussing labels, let me list some of the possible ones that can be hung around your neck as you age. For a man, "OLD COOT" comes to my mind first. I was working as a kitchen sales woman. The time was 1968. The elderly owner of the company had a reputation for being totally unapproachable, a fact that was well known by all the other employees but me. So from day one I always gave him a big smile and sunny good morning. The fact that I got a gruff, harrumph never dampened my effort to someday receive a good morning back, and I did . . . !

Diaries

I have a small cabinet that is almost filled with the diaries I have kept for the last thirty three years. Yesterday I opened the oldest one of them and began to read. In a very short time, I was transported to the year 1982, my daily record of the weather, my activities and my feelings on that day, that time, and moment. There were so many thing I had forgotten about the people and places, but most of all I lived it again, not as a fragmented memory but the reality of it just as I felt it and lived it. A diary is helpful in other ways too. It is a true understanding of the past as it happened. Bad feelings that are magnified by time, are not as bad as once were remembered. A renewed pleasure by reliving moments that should never be is a great addition to any day. Begin your record now so that someday when you are my age, you to will be glad you did. I am.

Now if you bought my book and have gotten to this page, I must first congratulate you on your adventurous nature. I am totally untrained in the correct way of doing many things, but I have found that to be an asset in the past. This became evident when I did many things successfully that I was told were impossible. It was because I didn't know what I was doing. Who decided what the rules were before they were written down by the right teacher, or cleric or any other know-it-all with some sort of degree? What I do know is a great deal more about living because I am an old lady. No one knows about that until they get to be old. So I have shared my experience with you in hopes that in some small way I have prepared you. I hope you are lucky enough to get there.

www.ingramcontent.com/pod-product-compliance
Lightning Source LLC
Chambersburg PA
CBHW082040080526
44578CB00009B/793